A
READER'S
JOURNAL

A
READER'S
JOURNAL

PROSPERO
B·O·O·K·S
A DIVISION OF CHAPTERS INC.

ISBN 1-55110-697-3
© Copyright 1997 held by   Chapters Inc.
                            90 Ronson Drive
                            Etobicoke, Ontario
                            M9W 1C1

This edition produced for Prospero Books,
a division of Chapters Inc.
by Waterlane Editions
Vancouver, Toronto

Printed and bound in Canada by Friesens, Altona, Manitoba.

Canadian Cataloguing in Publication Data
      Main entry under title:

      A reader's diary

            Co-published by: Prospero Books.
      ISBN 1-55110-698-1 (Waterlane) – ISBN 1-55110-697-3 (Prospero)

      1. Books and reading. 2. Diaries (Blank-books)
PN4395.R42 1997   O28'.9   C97-910692-3

TABLE OF CONTENTS

For one who reads, there is no limit to the number of lives that may be lived, for fiction, biography, and history offer an inexhaustible number of lives in many parts of the world, in all periods of time.

Louis L'Amour (1908-88)

W here is human nature so weak as in the bookstore!
Henry Ward Beecher (1813-87)

Without books, history is silent, literature dumb, science crippled, thought and speculation at a standstill.

Barbara Tuchman (1912-89)

When writers die they become books, which is, afterall, not too bad an incarnation.

Jorge Luis Borges (1899-1986)

The only books that influence us are those for which
we are ready, and which have gone a little farther
down our particular path than we have yet got ourselves.

E.M. Forster (1879-1970)

A bad book is as much a labour
to write as a good book.
Aldous Huxley (1894-1963)

T here is only one trait that marks the writer. He is always watching. It's a kind of trick of the mind and he is born with it.

Morley Callaghan (1903-90)

There is no money in poetry, but then there's no poetry in money either.

Robert Graves (1895-1985)

A ROOM OF ONE'S OWN

where we record the books we would like to add to our personal library

title

author

publisher/pub. date

notes

title

author

publisher/pub. date

notes

title

author

publisher/pub. date

notes

title

author

publisher/pub. date

notes

As sheer casual reading matter, I still find the English dictionary the most interesting book in our language.

Albert Jay Nock (1873-1945)

title

author

publisher/pub.date

notes

title

author

publisher/pub.date

notes

title

author

publisher/pub.date

notes

title

author

publisher/pub.date

notes

title

author

publisher/pub.date

notes

title
_____

author
_____

publisher/pub. date
_____

notes
_____
_____

title
_____

author
_____

publisher/pub. date
_____

notes
_____
_____

title
_____

author
_____

publisher/pub. date
_____

notes
_____
_____

title
_____

author
_____

publisher/pub. date
_____

notes
_____
_____

title
_____

author
_____

publisher/pub. date
_____

notes
_____
_____

title

author

publisher/pub.date

notes

title

author

publisher/pub.date

notes

title

author

publisher/pub.date

notes

title

author

publisher/pub.date

notes

title

author

publisher/pub.date

notes

title
_____

author
_____

publisher/pub. date
_____

notes
_____

title
_____

author
_____

publisher/pub. date
_____

notes
_____

title
_____

author
_____

publisher/pub. date
_____

notes
_____

title
_____

author
_____

publisher/pub. date
_____

notes
_____

title
_____

author
_____

publisher/pub. date
_____

notes
_____

F undamentally, all writing is about the same thing: it's about dying, about the brief flicker of time we have here, and the frustration that it creates.

Mordecai Richler (1931-)

title

author

publisher/pub.date

notes

title

author

publisher/pub.date

notes

title

author

publisher/pub.date

notes

title

author

publisher/pub.date

notes

title _____

author _____

publisher/pub.date _____

notes _____

title _____

author _____

publisher/pub.date _____

notes _____

title _____

author _____

publisher/pub.date _____

notes _____

title _____

author _____

publisher/pub.date _____

notes _____

title _____

author _____

publisher/pub.date _____

notes _____

title
_____

author
_____

publisher/pub.date
_____

notes
_____

title
_____

author
_____

publisher/pub.date
_____

notes
_____

title
_____

author
_____

publisher/pub.date
_____

notes
_____

title
_____

author
_____

publisher/pub.date
_____

notes
_____

All good books have one thing in common – they are truer than if they had really happened, and after you've read one of them you will feel that all that happened, happened to you and that it belongs to you forever....

Ernest Hemingway (1899-1961)

title

author

publisher/pub. date

notes

title

author

publisher/pub. date

notes

title

author

publisher/pub. date

notes

title

author

publisher/pub. date

notes

title

author

date and place read

notes

title

author

date and place read

notes

title

author

date and place read

notes

 ome books are to be tasted, others to be swallowed, and some to be chewed and digested.

Francis Bacon (1561-1626)

title

author

date and place read

notes

title

author

date and place read

notes

title

author

date and place read

notes

title

author

date and place read

notes

title

author

date and place read

notes

title

author

date and place read

notes

L iterature is my Utopia. Here I am not disfranchised. No barrier of the senses shuts me out from the sweet, gracious discourse of my book friends. They talk to me without embarrassment or awkwardness.

Helen Keller (1880-1968)

title

author

date and place read

notes

title

author

date and place read

notes

title

author

date and place read

notes

title

author

date and place read

notes

title

author

date and place read

notes

title

author

date and place read

notes

title

author

date and place read

notes

title

author

date and place read

notes

title

author

date and place read

notes

title

author

date and place read

notes

title

author

date and place read

notes

title

author

date and place read

notes

title

author

date and place read

notes

title

author

date and place read

notes

 great writer is the friend and benefactor of his readers.
Thomas Babington Macaulay (1800-59)

title

author

date and place read

notes

title

author

date and place read

notes

title

author

date and place read

notes

title

author

date and place read

notes

title

author

date and place read

notes

title

author

date and place read

notes

title

author

date and place read

notes

title

author

date and place read

notes

title

author

date and place read

notes

Everything in the world exists to end up in a book.
Stéphane Mallarmé (1842-98)

title

author

date and place read

notes

title

author

date and place read

notes

title

author

date and place read

notes

title

author

date and place read

notes

title

author

date and place read

notes

title

author

date and place read

notes

L iterature is where I go to explore the highest and lowest places in human society and in the human spirit, where I hope to find out not the absolute truth but the truth of the tale, of the imagination and of the heart.

Salman Rushdie (1947-)

title

author

date and place read

notes

title

author

date and place read

notes

title

author

date and place read

notes

title

author

date and place read

notes

title

author

date and place read

notes

title

author

date and place read

notes

title

author

date and place read

notes

title

author

date and place read

notes

title

author

date and place read

notes

title

author

date and place read

notes

title

author

date and place read

notes

 hile thought exists, words are alive and literature
becomes an escape, not from, but into living.

Cyril Connolly (1903-74)

title

author

date and place read

notes

---

title

author

date and place read

notes   .

---

title

author

date and place read

notes

title

author

date and place read

notes

title

author

date and place read

notes

title

author

date and place read

notes

title

author

date and place read

notes

title

author

date and place read

notes

title

author

date and place read

notes

Writing is no trouble: you just jot down ideas as they occur to you. The jotting is simplicity itself – it is the occurring which is difficult.

Stephen Leacock (1869-1944)

title

author

date and place read

notes

title

author

date and place read

notes

title

author

date and place read

notes

title

author

date and place read

notes

title

author

date and place read

notes

title

author

date and place read

notes

title

author

date and place read

notes

title

author

date and place read

notes

title

author

date and place read

notes

title

author

date and place read

notes

title

author

date and place read

notes

title

author

date and place read

notes

title

author

date and place read

notes

title

author

date and place read

notes

title

author

date and place read

notes

 book is solitude, privacy; it is a way of holding the self apart from the crush of the outer world.

Sven Birkerts (1951-)

title

author

date and place read

notes

title

author

date and place read

notes

title

author

date and place read

notes

title

author

date and place read

notes

title

author

date and place read

notes

title

author

date and place read

notes

title _____

author _____

date and place read _____

notes _____

_____

_____

_____

_____

title _____

author _____

date and place read _____

notes _____

_____

_____

_____

_____

title _____

author _____

date and place read _____

notes _____

I t is a great thing to start life with a small number of really good books which are your very own.

Sir Arthur Conan Doyle (1859-1930)

title

author

date and place read

notes

title

author

date and place read

notes

title

author

date and place read

notes

title

author

date and place read

notes

title

author

date and place read

notes

EX LIBRIS

KIDNAPPED

in which we find lists of books
we have borrowed and those borrowed from us

title

author

borrowed from

date borrowed

date returned

title

author

borrowed from

date borrowed

date returned

title

author

borrowed from

date borrowed

date returned

title

author

borrowed from

date borrowed

date returned

A room without books is like a body without soul.
Marcus Tullius Cicero (106-43 BC)

title

author

borrowed from

date borrowed

date returned

title

author

borrowed from

date borrowed

date returned

title

author

borrowed from

date borrowed

date returned

title

author

borrowed from

date borrowed

date returned

title

author

borrowed from

date borrowed

date returned

title

author

borrowed from

date borrowed

date returned

title

author

borrowed from

date borrowed

date returned

title

author

borrowed from

date borrowed

date returned

title

author

borrowed from

date borrowed

date returned

title

author

borrowed from

date borrowed

date returned

riends can betray you but books are always loyal.

Wang Gho Zhen

title

author

borrowed from

date borrowed

date returned

title

author

borrowed from

date borrowed

date returned

title

author

borrowed from

date borrowed

date returned

title

author

borrowed from

date borrowed

date returned

title

author

borrowed from

date borrowed

date returned

title

author

borrowed from

date borrowed

date returned

title

author

borrowed from

date borrowed

date returned

title

author

borrowed from

date borrowed

date returned

title

author

borrowed by

date borrowed

date returned

title

author

borrowed by

date borrowed

date returned

title

author

borrowed by

date borrowed

date returned

Every man who knows how to read has it in his power to magnify himself, to multiply the ways in which he exists, to make his life full, significant and interesting.

Aldous Huxley (1894-1963)

title

author

borrowed by

date borrowed

date returned

title

author

borrowed by

date borrowed

date returned

title

author

borrowed by

date borrowed

date returned

title

author

borrowed by

date borrowed

date returned

title

author

borrowed by

date borrowed

date returned

title

author

borrowed by

date borrowed

date returned

title

author

borrowed by

date borrowed

date returned

title

author

borrowed by

date borrowed

date returned

title

author

borrowed by

date borrowed

date returned

title

author

borrowed by

date borrowed

date returned

title

author

borrowed by

date borrowed

date returned

title

author

borrowed by

date borrowed

date returned

title

author

borrowed by

date borrowed

date returned

title

author

borrowed by

date borrowed

date returned

title

author

borrowed by

date borrowed

date returned

title

author

borrowed by

date borrowed

date returned

I have always come to life after coming to books.
Jorge Luis Borges (1899-1986)

title

author

borrowed by

date borrowed

date returned

title

author

borrowed by

date borrowed

date returned

title

author

borrowed by

date borrowed

date returned

title

author

borrowed by

date borrowed

date returned

title

author

borrowed by

date borrowed

date returned

title

author

borrowed by

date borrowed

date returned

title

author

borrowed by

date borrowed

date returned

FATHERS AND SONS

in which we find lists of books to give
as gifts and those books given to us

give to

title

author

occasion

give to

title

author

occasion

give to

title

author

occasion

give to

title

author

occasion

I f you caricature friends in your first novel they will be upset, but if you don't they will feel betrayed.

Mordecai Richler (1931-)

give to

title

author

occasion

give to

title

author

occasion

give to

title

author

occasion

give to

title

author

occasion

give to

title

author

occasion

give to

title

author

occasion

give to

title

author

occasion

give to

title

author

occasion

give to

title

author

occasion

give to

title

author

occasion

give to
_____

title
_____

author
_____

occasion
_____

give to
_____

title
_____

author
_____

occasion
_____

give to
_____

title
_____

author
_____

occasion
_____

give to
_____

title
_____

author
_____

occasion
_____

give to
_____

title
_____

author
_____

occasion
_____

Books are not rolls, to be devoured only when they are hot and fresh. A good book retains its interior heat and will warm a generation yet unborn.

Clifton Fadiman (1904-)

give to

title

author

occasion

give to

title

author

occasion

give to

title

author

occasion

give to

title

author

occasion

give to

title

author

occasion

give to

title

author

occasion

give to

title

author

occasion

give to

title

author

occasion

give to

title

author

occasion

give to

title

author

occasion

give to

title

author

occasion

give to

title

author

occasion

give to

title

author

occasion

give to

title

author

occasion

give to

title

author

occasion

give to

title

author

occasion

give to

title

author

occasion

give to

title

author

occasion

give to

title

author

occasion

give to

title

author

occasion

give to

title

author

occasion

give to

title

author

occasion

give to

title

author

occasion

give to

title

author

occasion

I wish thee as much pleasure in the reading,
as I had in the writing.

Francis Quarles (1592-1644)

give to

title

author

occasion

give to

title

author

occasion

give to

title

author

occasion

give to

title

author

occasion

given by

title

author

occasion

given by

title

author

occasion

given by

title

author

occasion

given by

title

author

occasion

given by

title

author

occasion

given by

title

author

occasion

given by

title

author

occasion

given by

title

author

occasion

given by

title

author

occasion

given by

title

author

occasion

give to

title

author

occasion

give to

title

author

occasion

give to

title

author

occasion

give to

title

author

occasion

When I am dead, I hope it may be said:
'His sins were scarlet, but his books were read.'
Hilaire Belloc (1870-1953)

given by

title

author

occasion

given by

title

author

occasion

given by

title

author

occasion

given by

title

author

occasion

given by

title

author

occasion

given by

title

author

occasion

given by

title

author

occasion

given by

title

author

occasion

given by

title

author

occasion

given by

title

author

occasion

given by

title

author

occasion

given by

title

author

occasion

given by

title

author

occasion

given by

title

author

occasion

given by

title

author

occasion

'**T**is the good reader that makes the good book.
Ralph Waldo Emerson (1803-82)

give to _____

title _____

author _____

occasion _____

give to _____

title _____

author _____

occasion _____

give to _____

title _____

author _____

occasion _____

give to _____

title _____

author _____

occasion _____

WHEN WE WERE VERY YOUNG

*in which we remember our favourite
children's books, from youth and adulthood*

> **T**here are only two or three human stories,
> and they go on repeating themselves as
> fiercely as if they had never happened before.
> *Willa Cather (1873-1974)*

ON THE ROAD

in which we find a collection of books
suited for holidays, beaches and buses

I never travel without my diary.
One should always have something
sensational to read in the train.

Oscar Wilde (1854-1900)

Reading is to the mind what exercise is to the body.

Sir Richard Steele (1672-1759)

EX LIBRIS

FAR FROM THE MADDING CROWD

in which we make note of book festivals,
author readings and other events for readers

Reading is the work of an alert mind,
is demanding, and under ideal conditions
produces finally a sort of ecstasy.

E.B. White (1899-1985)

event

date/place

notes

event

date/place

notes

event

date/place

notes

event

date/place

notes

event

date/place

notes

event

date/place

notes

event

date/place

notes

event

date/place

notes

event

date/place

notes

event
_____

date/place
_____

notes
_____
_____
_____

event
_____

date/place
_____

notes
_____
_____
_____

event
_____

date/place
_____

notes
_____
_____
_____

event
_____

date/place
_____

notes
_____
_____
_____

event
_____

date/place
_____

notes
_____
_____
_____

This is the Great Theatre of Life. Admission is free but the taxation is mortal. You come when you can, and leave when you must. The show is continuous. Good-night.

Robertson Davies (1913-95) from The Cunning Man

event

date/place

notes

event

date/place

notes

event

date/place

notes

event

date/place

notes

event

date/place

notes

event

date/place

notes

event

date/place

notes

event

date/place

notes

event

date/place

notes

A CIRCLE
OF FRIENDS

in which we find a list of members of our reading club,
lists of books to read in a group and the thoughts
of the group on books read

member	phone number	address

title   author

meeting date/time/place

title

author

members

notes

The liveliness of literature lies in its exceptionality, in being the individual, idiosyncratic vision of one human being, in which, to our delight and great surprise, we may find our own vision reflected.

Salman Rushdie (1947-)

meeting date/time/place

title

author

members

notes

meeting date/time/place

title

author

members

notes

meeting date/time/place

title

author

members

notes

meeting date/time/place

title

author

members

notes

meeting date/time/place

title

author

members

notes

The only important thing in a book is
the meaning it has for you.
W. Somerset Maugham (1874-1965)

meeting date/time/place

title

author

members

notes

meeting date/time/place

title

author

members

notes

meeting date/time/place

title

author

members

notes

There are worse crimes than burning books.
One of them is not reading them.

Joseph Brodsky (1940-)

meeting date/time/place

title

author

members

notes

meeting date/time/place

title

author

members

notes

THE MERCHANT OF VENICE

*in which we find addresses of bookstores,
libraries, and book-loving friends*

name
—————————————————————————————————————

address
—————————————————————————————————————

phone
—————————————————————————————————————

notes
—————————————————————————————————————

name
—————————————————————————————————————

address
—————————————————————————————————————

phone
—————————————————————————————————————

notes
—————————————————————————————————————

name
—————————————————————————————————————

address
—————————————————————————————————————

phone
—————————————————————————————————————

notes
—————————————————————————————————————

name
—————————————————————————————————————

address
—————————————————————————————————————

phone
—————————————————————————————————————

notes
—————————————————————————————————————

The magic of a bookstore stems in part from the depth of literature it contains, its surprises and mysteries ... A magical store has its own character and spirit.

Thomas Moore (1940-)

name

address

phone

notes

name

address

phone

notes

name

address

phone

notes

name

address

phone

notes

name

address

phone

notes

name

address

phone

notes

name

address

phone

notes

name

address

phone

notes

name

address

phone

notes

name

address

phone

notes

name

address

phone

notes

name

address

phone

notes

name

address

phone

notes

name

address

phone

notes

name

address

phone

notes

W ith thought, patience, and discrimination, book passion becomes the signature of a person's character.

Nicholas A. Basbanes, A Gentle Madness

name

address

phone

notes

name

address

phone

notes

name

address

phone

notes

name

address

phone

notes

FAMOUS
LAST WORDS
in which we record memorable quotations
from favourite books and authors

A.W. TOZER :   What we believe about God is
the most important thing about us

Meeting Lily: ...he rushed her away to Italy &
the green hill & the villa "and the sun" said Aunt
Dot, who believed implicitly in its healing powers.

The role of the writer is not to say what we
can all say, but what we are unable to say.

Anaïs Nin (1903-77)